how
to
bring up
a child ?

"Children are the hope of the Future, the builders of tomorrow." How often have these words been quoted and requoted! And one cannot deny that, in modern times, efforts have also been made to bring children up in the proper way and to give them the right education. But most of our efforts have been gropings in the dark. We do not know what is a child. We do not understand him. We are ignorant of his deeper needs and inner movements. We are not aware of the true meaning of education.

This book is an attempt to bring some light into this obscure yet important field. The contents are grouped as follows :

- *A famous Chinese saying which presents beautifully the need for such a book.*
- *The principal section, formed of extracts from the writings of Sri Aurobindo and the Mother, which explore briefly various aspects of the Art and Science of*

dealing with children. The topics cover a wide range. There are sections on practical problems about the food and sleep of children. Others raise very fundamental questions : what is the only thing worth teaching? what is the most precious gift one can make to a child? There are extracts on situations which parents and teachers meet everyday, sometimes quite helplessly : what should one do when a child wants something and does not stop crying? when a child misbehaves in the class? when children want to play games with guns and swords? The answers given by the Mother are most practical and at the same time full of a deep spiritual insight.

- *Some reminiscences of those who had the privilege of observing the Mother's way of dealing with children _ a way of infinite love and understanding.*

- *A story from ancient India which raises the whole question of learning and the purpose of education : whether what we are now imparting can at all be considered as education when it does not tell us the nature of the Self and Reality; when it does not give us that Knowledge knowing which everything is known. It is the famous story of Svetaketu from the Chandogya Upanishad.*

- *Two simple and small anecdotes from the West. The first gives the story of a priest who was faced with an impossible child and the second is a sweet and touching story of the way in which an older person saved a child's dream-world from being shattered.*

This tiny book can in no way claim to present a comprehensive treatment of the subject. In fact, even from the Mother's words, some of the most important writings have been omitted. The stress, in this compilation, has been on practical suggestions about facing and handling situations which arise every day in the lives of those who are responsible for looking after children. Most of the observations made by the Mother can apply to children of all ages though they might have been made in the context of a particular child or age group.

We trust that this book will be a small but significant contribution to the growing literature on child psychology and act as a handbook for parents, guardians and teachers. We would also like to point out that truth is too vast and global to be encompassed in words, and this book should be used, not as a collection of rules to be applied ritually but as a torch to light the way.

When planning for a year —
sow corn.

When planning for a decade —
plant trees.

When planning for life —
train and educate men.

Kwan-Tsu

The Child

A SOUL MEANT TO GROW

The child was in the ancient patriarchal idea the live property of the father; he was his creation, his production, his own reproduction of himself; the father, rather than God or the universal Life in place of God, stood as the author of the child's being; and the creator has every right over his creation, the producer over his manufacture. He had the right to make of him what he willed, and not what the being of the child really was within, to train and shape and cut him according to the parental ideas and not rear him according to his own nature's deepest needs, to bind him to the paternal career or the career chosen by the parent and not that to which his nature and capacity and inclination pointed, to fix for him all the critical turning-points of his life even after he had reached maturity. In education the child was regarded not as a soul meant to grow, but as brute psychological stuff to be shaped into a fixed mould by the teacher. We have travelled to another conception of the child as a soul with a being, a nature and capacities of his own who must be helped to find them, to find himself, to grow into their maturity, into a fullness of physical and vital energy and the utmost breadth, depth, and height of his emotional, his intellectual and his spiritual being.

SRI AUROBINDO

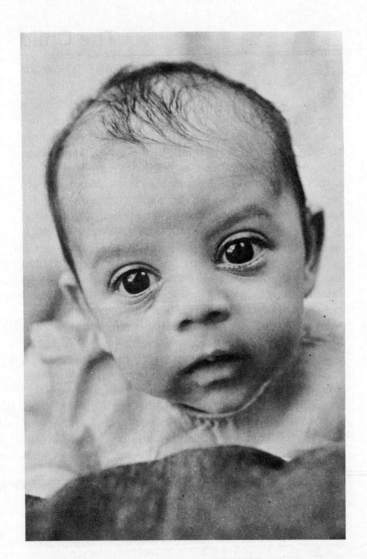

Education begins before Birth

To speak of children to the women of Japan is, I think, to speak to them of their dearest, their most sacred subject. Indeed, in no other country in the world have the children taken such an important, such a primordial place. They are, here, the centre of care and attention. On them are concentrated – and rightly – the hopes for the future. They are the living promise of growing prosperity for the country. Therefore, the most important work assigned to women in Japan is child-making. Maternity is considered as the principle role of woman. But this is true only so long as we understand what is meant by the word maternity. For to bring children into the world as rabbits do their young – instinctively, ignorantly, machine-like, that certainly cannot be called maternity! True maternity begins with the conscious creation of a being, with the willed shaping of a soul coming to develop and utilise a new body. The true domain of women is the spiritual. We forget it but too often.

To bear a child and construct his body almost subconsciously is not enough. The work really commences when, by the power of thought and will, we conceive and create a character capable of manifesting an ideal.

And do not say that we have no power for realising such a thing. Innumerable instances of this very effective power could be brought out as proofs.

First of all, the effect of physical environment was recognised and studied long ago. It is by surrounding women with forms of art and beauty that, little by little, the ancient Greeks created the exceptionally harmonious race that they were.

Individual instances of the same fact are numerous. It is not rare to see a woman who, while pregnant, had looked at constantly and admired a beautiful picture or statue, giving birth to a child after the perfect likeness of this picture or statue. I met several of these instances myself. Among them, I remember very clearly two little girls; they were twins and perfectly beautiful. But the most astonishing was how little like their parents they were. They reminded me of a very famous picture painted by the English artist Reynolds. One day I made this remark to the mother, who immediately exclaimed: "Indeed, is it not so? You will be interested to know that while I was expecting these children, I had, hanging above my bed, a very good reproduction of Reynolds' picture. Before going to sleep and as soon as I woke, my last and first glance was for that picture; and in my heart I hoped: may my children be like the faces in this picture. You see that I succeeded quite well!" In truth, she could be proud of her success, and her example is of great utility for other women.

But if we can obtain such results on the physical plane where the materials are the least plastic, how much more so on the psychological plane where the influence of thought and will is so powerful. Why accept the obscure bonds of heredity and atavism – which are nothing else than subconscious preferences for our own trend of character – when we can, by concentration and will, call into being a type constructed according to the highest ideal we are able to conceive? With this effort, maternity becomes truly precious and sacred; indeed with this, we enter the glorious work of the Spirit, and womanhood rises above animality and its ordinary instincts, towards real humanity and its powers.

In this effort, in this attempt, then, lies our true duty.

And if this was always of the greatest importance, it certainly has taken a capital one in the present turn of the earth's evolution.

*

The education of a human being should begin at birth and continue throughout his life.

Indeed, if we want this education to have its maximum result, it should begin even before birth; in this case it is the mother herself who proceeds with this education by means of a twofold action: first, upon herself for her own improvement, and secondly, upon the child whom she is forming physically. For it is certain that the nature of the child to be born depends very much upon the mother who forms it, upon her aspirations and will as well as upon the material surroundings in which she lives. To see that her thoughts are always beautiful and pure, her feelings always noble and fine, her material surroundings as harmonious as possible and full of a great simplicity – this is the part of education which should apply to the mother herself. And if she has in addition a conscious and definite will to form the child according to the highest ideal she can conceive, then the very best conditions will be realised so that the child can come into the world with his utmost potentialities. How many difficult efforts and useless complications would be avoided in this way!

THE MOTHER

To Educate a Child is to Educate Oneself

Most parents, for various reasons, give very little thought to the true education which should be imparted to children. When they have brought a child into the world, provided him with food, satisfied his various material needs and looked after his health more or less carefully, they think they have fully discharged their duty. Later on, they will send him to school and hand over to the teachers the responsibility for his education.

There are other parents who know that their children must be educated and who try to do what they can. But very few, even among those who are most serious and sincere, know that the first thing to do, in order to be able to educate a child, is to educate oneself, to become conscious and master of oneself so that one never sets a bad example to one's child. For it is above all through example that education becomes effective. To speak good words and to give wise advice to a child has very little effect if one does not oneself give him an example of what one teaches. Sincerity, honesty, straightforwardness, courage, disinterestedness, unselfishness, patience, endurance, perseverance, peace, calm, self-control are all things that are taught infinitely better by example than by beautiful speeches. Parents, have a high ideal and always act in accordance with it and you will see that little by little your child will reflect this ideal in himself and spontaneously manifest the qualities you would like to see expressed in his nature. Quite naturally a child has respect and admiration for his parents; unless they are quite unworthy, they will always appear to their child as demigods whom he will try to imitate as best he can.

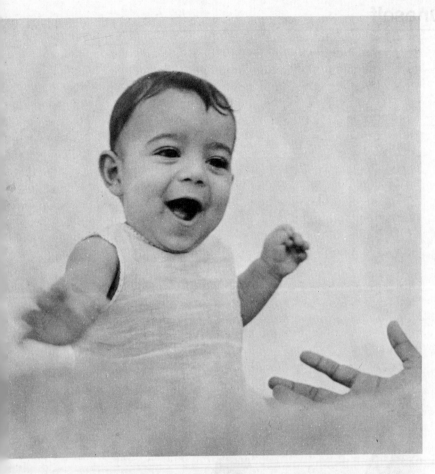

yourself and be worthy of respect at every moment. Never be authoritarian, despotic, impatient or ill-tempered. When your child asks you a question, do not give him a stupid or silly answer under the pretext that he cannot understand you. You can always make yourself understood if you take enough trouble; and in spite of the popular saying that it is always good to tell the truth, I affirm that it is always good to tell the truth, but that the art consists in telling it in such a way as to make it accessible to the mind of the hearer. In early life, until he is twelve or fourteen, the child's mind is hardly open to abstract notions and general ideas. And yet you can train it to understand these things by using concrete images, symbols or parables. Up to quite an advanced age and for some who mentally always remain children, a narrative, a story, a tale well told teach much more than any number of theoretical explanations.

*

The worst of all (which men usually do) is to leave their children with servants. It is a crime.... Naturally, there is also the age when children are put to school and there they begin to come in contact with a host of children who are not always very much to be recommended. It is very difficult to escape these relations. But all the same, if one has started life with a little consciousness and much goodwill, when one meets people who are not desirable company, one feels it. And if one is goodwilled, immediately one tries not to see them or not to be with them.

With very few exceptions, parents are not aware of the disastrous influence that their own defects, impulses, weaknesses and lack of self-control have on their children. If you wish to be respected by a child, have respect for

For a Body fit to manifest Beauty

I have said that from a young age children should be taught to respect good health, physical strength and balance. The great importance of beauty must also be emphasised. A young child should aspire for beauty, not for the sake of pleasing others or winning their admiration, but for the love of beauty itself; for beauty is the ideal which all physical life must realise. Every human being has the possibility of establishing harmony among the different parts of his body and in the various movements of the body in action. Every human body that undergoes a rational method of culture from the very beginning of its existence can realise its own harmony and thus become fit to manifest beauty....

So far I have referred only to the education to be given to children; for a good many bodily defects can be rectified and many malformations avoided by an enlightened physical education given at the proper time. But if for any reason this physical education has not been given during childhood or even in youth, it can begin at any age and be pursued throughout life. But the later one begins, the more one must be prepared to meet bad habits that have to be corrected, rigidities to be made supple, malformations to be rectified. And this preparatory work will require much patience and perseverance before one can start on a constructive programme for the harmonisation of the form and its movements. But if you keep alive within you the ideal of beauty that is to be realised, sooner or later you are sure to reach the goal you have set yourself.

THE MOTHER

All education of the body, if it is to be effective, must be rigorous and detailed, far-sighted and methodical. This will be translated into habits; the body is a being of habits. But these habits should be controlled and disciplined, while remaining flexible enough to adapt themselves to circumstances and to the needs of the growth and development of the being.

All education of the body should begin at birth and continue throughout life. It is never too soon to begin nor too late to continue.

Physical education has three principal aspects: (1) control and discipline of the functioning of the body, (2) an integral, methodical and harmonious development of all the parts and movements of the body and (3) correction of any defects and deformities.

It may be said that from the very first days, even the first hours of his life, the child should undergo the first part of this programme as far as food, sleep, evacuation, etc. are concerned. If the child, from the very beginning of his existence, learns good habits, it will save him a good deal of trouble and inconvenience for the rest of his life; and besides, those who have the responsibility of caring for him during his first years will find their task very much easier.

Naturally, this education, if it is to be rational, enlightened and effective, must be based upon a minimum knowledge of the human body, of its structure and its functioning. As the child develops, he must gradually be taught to observe the functioning of his internal organs so that he may control them more and more, and see that this functioning remains normal and harmonious. As for positions, postures and movements, bad habits are formed very early and very rapidly, and these may have disastrous consequences for his whole life. Those who take the question of

physical education seriously and wish to give their children the best conditions for normal development will easily find the necessary indications and instructions. The subject is being more and more thoroughly studied, and many books have appeared and are still appearing which give all the information and guidance needed.

FOOD AND THE BODY'S NEEDS

The question of food has been studied at length and in detail; the diet that helps children in their growth is generally known and it may be very useful to follow it. But it is very important to remember that the instinct of the body, so long as it remains intact, is more reliable than any theory. Accordingly, those who want their child to develop normally should not force him to eat food which he finds distasteful, for most often the body possesses a sure instinct as to what is harmful to it, unless the child is particularly capricious.

The body in its normal state, that is to say, when there is no intervention of mental notions or vital impulses, also knows very well what is good and necessary for it; but for this to be effective in practice, one must educate the child with care and teach him to distinguish his desires from his needs. He should be helped to develop a taste for food that is simple and healthy, substantial and appetising, but free from any useless complications. In his daily food, all that merely stuffs and causes heaviness should be avoided; and above all, he must be taught to eat according to his hunger, neither more nor less, and not to make his meals an occasion to satisfy his greed or gluttony. From one's very childhood, one should know that one eats in order to give

strength and health to the body and not to enjoy the pleasures of the palate. Children should be given food that suits their temperament, prepared in a way that ensures hygiene and cleanliness, that is pleasant to the taste and yet very simple. This food should be chosen and apportioned according to the age of the child and his regular activities. It should contain all the chemical and dynamic elements that are necessary for his development and the balanced growth of every part of his body.

Since the child will be given only the food that helps to keep him healthy and provide him with the energy he needs, one must be very careful not to use food as a means of coercion and punishment. The practice of telling a child, "You have not been a good boy, you won't get any dessert," etc., is most harmful. In this way you create in his little consciousness the impression that food is given to him chiefly to satisfy his greed and not because it is indispensable for the proper functioning of his body.

IMPORTANCE OF SLEEP

A child, whatever his activities, should have a sufficient number of hours of sleep. The number will vary according to his age. In the cradle, the baby should sleep longer than he remains awake. The number of hours of sleep will diminish as the child grows. But until maturity it should not be less than eight hours, in a quiet, well-ventilated place. The child should never be made to stay up late for no reason. The hours before midnight are the best for resting the nerves. Even during the waking hours, relaxation is indispensable for all who want to maintain their nervous balance. To know how to relax the muscles and the nerves **15** is an art which should be taught to children when they are very young. There are many parents who, on the contrary, push their child to constant activity. When the child remains quiet, they imagine that he is ill. There are even parents who have the bad habit of making their child do household work at the expense of his rest and relaxation. Nothing is worse for a developing nervous system, which cannot stand the strain of too continuous an effort or of an activity that is imposed upon it and not freely chosen. At the risk of going against many current ideas and ruffling many prejudices, I hold that it is not fair to demand service from a child, as if it were his duty to serve his parents. The contrary would be more true, and certainly it is natural that parents should serve their child or at least take great care of him. It is only if a child chooses freely to work for his family and does this work as play that the thing is admissible. And even then, one must be careful that it in no way diminishes the hours of rest that are absolutely indispensable for his body to function properly.

*

Q: *Sometimes, Mother, when children are interested in something, they don't want to go to bed, then what should be done? Just a few minutes earlier they said they were sleepy, and then they start playing and say they don't want to go to bed.*

They shouldn't be allowed to play when they are sleepy. This is exactly the intrusion of vital movements. A child who doesn't live much with older people (it is bad for children to live much among older people), a child left to itself will sleep spontaneously whatever it may be doing, the moment it needs to sleep. Only, when children are used

to living with older people, well, they catch all the habits of the grown-ups. Specially when they are told: "Oh! you can't do this because you are young! When you are older, you can do it. You can't eat this because you are small, when you are bigger you will be able to eat it. At this particular time you must go to bed because you are young...." So, naturally, they have that idea that they must grow up at any cost or at least look grown-up!

RESPECT HEALTH AND CLEANLINESS

Another thing should be taught to a child from his early years: to enjoy cleanliness and observe hygienic habits. But, in obtaining this cleanliness and respect for the rules of hygiene from the child, one must take great care not to instil into him the fear of illness. Fear is the worst instrument of education and the surest way of attracting what is feared. Yet, while there should be no fear of illness, there should be no inclination for it either. There is a prevalent belief that brilliant minds are found in weak bodies. This is a delusion and has no basis. There was perhaps a time when a romantic and morbid taste for physical unbalance prevailed; but, fortunately, that tendency has disappeared. Nowadays a well-built, robust, muscular, strong and well-balanced body is appreciated at its true value. In any case, children should be taught to respect health and admire the healthy man whose vigorous body knows how to repel attacks of illness. Often a child feigns illness to avoid some troublesome obligation, a work that does not interest him, or simply to soften his parents' hearts and get them to satisfy some caprice. The child must be taught as early as possible that this does not work and that he does not become more interesting by being ill, but rather the contrary. The weak have a tendency to believe that their weakness makes them particularly interesting and to use this weakness and if necessary even illness as a means of attracting the attention and sympathy of the people around them. On no account should this pernicious tendency be encouraged. Children should therefore be taught that to be ill is a sign of weakness and inferiority, not of some virtue or sacrifice.

SPORTS AND SPORTSMANSHIP

As soon as the child is able to make use of his limbs, some time should be devoted every day to the methodical and regular development of all the parts of his body. Every day some twenty or thirty minutes, preferably on waking, if possible, will be enough to ensure the proper functioning and balanced growth of his muscles while preventing any stiffening of the joints and of the spine, which occurs much sooner than one thinks. In the general programme of the child's education, sports and outdoor games should be given a prominent place; that, more than all the medicines in the world, will assure the child good health. An hour's moving about in the sun does more to cure weakness or even anæmia than a whole arsenal of tonics. My advice is that medicines should not be used unless it is absolutely impossible to avoid them; and this "absolutely impossible" should be very strict. In this programme of physical culture, although there are well-known general lines to be followed for the best development of the human body, still, if the method is to be fully effective in each case, it should be considered individually, if possible with the help of a competent person, or if not, by consulting the numerous manuals that have already been and are still being published on the subject.

*

Q: *Sweet Mother, during our tournaments there are many who play in a very bad spirit. They try to hurt others in order to win. And we have noticed that even the little ones are learning to do this. How could it be avoided?*

With children it is above all ignorance and bad example which cause the harm. So it would be good if, before they begin their games, all the group-leaders, the captains, call together all those they are in charge of and tell them, explain to them exactly what Sri Aurobindo says here, with detailed explanations like those we have given in the two little books *The Code of Sportmanship* and *The Ideal Child* [*What a Child Should Always Remember*]. These things must be repeated often to the children. And then, you must warn them against bad company, bad friends, as I told you in another class.

And above all, set them the right example....Be yourself what you would like them to be. Give them the example of disinterestedness, patience, self-control, constant good humour, the overcoming of one's little personal dislikes, a sort of constant goodwill, an understanding of others' difficulties; and that equality of temper which makes children free from fear, for what makes children deceitful and untruthful, and even cunning, is the fear of being punished. If they feel secure, they will hide nothing and you will then be able to help them to be loyal and honest. Of all things the most important is good example. Sri Aurobindo speaks of that, of the invariable good humour one must have in all circumstances, this self-forgetfulness: not to throw one's own little troubles on others; when one is tired or uncomfortable, not to become unpleasant, impatient. This asks for quite some perfection, a self-control which is a great step on the path of realisation. If one fulfilled the conditions needed to be a true leader, even if only a leader of a small group of children, well, one would already be far advanced in the discipline needed for the accomplishment of the yoga.

THE MOTHER

Teacher – a Living Example

PERSONALITY TRAITS OF A SUCCESSFUL TEACHER

1. Complete self-control not only to the extent of not showing any anger, but remaining absolutely quiet and undisturbed under all circumstances.

2. In the matter of self-confidence, must also have a sense of the relativity of his importance.

Above all, must have the knowledge that the teacher himself must always progress if he wants his students to progress, must not remain satisfied either with what he is or with what he knows.

3. Must not have any sense of essential superiority over his students nor preference or attachment whatsoever for one or another.

4. Must know that all are equal spiritually and instead of mere tolerance must have a global comprehension or understanding.

5. "The business of both parent and teacher is to enable and to help the child to educate himself, to develop his own intellectual, moral, aesthetic and practical capacities and to grow freely as an organic being, not to be kneaded and pressured into form like an inert plastic material."

The interest of the students is proportionate to the *true capacity* of the teacher.

THE MOTHER

There is no better lesson than that of an example. To tell others: "Do not be selfish," is not much use, but if somebody is free from all selfishness, he becomes a wonderful example to others; and someone who sincerely aspires to act in accordance with the Supreme Truth, creates a kind of contagion for the people around him. So the first duty of all those who are teachers or instructors is to give an example of the qualities they teach to others.

And if, among these teachers and instructors, some are not worthy of their post, because by their character they give a bad example, their first duty is to become worthy by changing their character and their action; there is no other way.

*

Example is the most powerful instructor. Never demand from a child an effort of discipline that you do not make yourself. Calm, equanimity, order, method, absence of useless words, ought to be constantly practised by the teacher if he wants to instil them into his pupils.

The teacher should always be punctual and come to the class a few minutes before it begins, always properly dressed. And above all, so that his students should never lie, he must never lie himself; so that his students should never lose their tempers, he should never lose his temper with them; and to have the right to say to them, "Rough play often ends in tears", he should never raise his hand against any of them.

These are elementary and preliminary things which ought to be practised in all schools without exception.

To Teach in the Right Way

Every child is a lover of interesting narrative, a hero-worshipper and a patriot. Appeal to these qualities in him and through them let him master without knowing it the living and human parts of his nation's history. Every child is an inquirer, an investigator, analyser, a merciless anatomist. Appeal to these qualities in him and let him acquire without knowing it the right temper and the necessary fundamental knowledge of the scientist. Every child has an insatiable intellectual curiosity and turn for metaphysical enquiry. Use it to draw him on slowly to an understanding of the world and himself. Every child has the gift of imitation and a touch of imaginative power. Use it to give him the ground-work of the faculty of the artist.

SRI AUROBINDO

Most teachers want to have *good students*: students who are studious and attentive, who understand and know many things, who can answer well – good students. This spoils everything. The students begin to consult books, to study, to learn. Then they rely only on books, on what others say or write, and they lose contact with the superconscient part which receives knowledge by intuition. This contact often exists in a small child but it is lost in the course of his education.

THE MOTHER

There is one thing that I must emphasise. Don't try to follow what is done in the universities outside. Don't try to pump into the students mere data and information. Don't give them so much work that they may not get time for anything else. You are not in a great hurry to catch a train. Let the students understand what they learn. Let them assimilate it. Finishing the course should not be your goal. You should make the programme in such a way that the students may get time to attend the subjects they want to learn. They should have sufficient time for their physical exercises. I don't want them to be very good students, yet pale, thin, anaemic. Perhaps you will say that in this way they will not have sufficient time for their studies, but that can be made up by expanding the course over a longer period. Instead of finishing a course in four years, you can take six years. Rather it would be better for them; they will be able to assimilate more of the atmosphere here and their progress will not be just in one direction at the cost of everything else. It will be an all-round progress in all directions.

What you should do is to teach the children to take interest in what they are doing – that is not the same thing as interesting the students! You must arouse in them the desire for knowledge, for progress. One can take an interest in anything – in sweeping a room, for example – if one does it with concentration, in order to gain an experience, to make a progress, to become more conscious. I often say this to the students who complain of having a bad teacher. Even if they don't like the teacher, even if he tells them useless things or if he is not up to the mark, they can always derive some benefit from their period of class, learn something of great interest and progress in consciousness.

*

It would be interesting to formulate or to elaborate a new method of teaching for children, to take them very young. It is easy when they are very young. We need people – oh! we would need remarkable teachers – who have, first, an ample enough documentation of what is known so as to be able to answer every question, and at the same time, at least the knowledge, if not the experience – the experience would be better – of the true intuitive intellectual attitude, and – naturally the capacity would be still more preferable – at least the knowledge that the true way of knowing is mental silence, an attentive silence turned towards the truer Consciousness, and the capacity to receive what comes from there. The best would be to have this capacity; at least, it should be explained that it is the true thing – a sort of demonstration – and that it works not only from the point of view of what must be learned, of the whole domain of knowledge, but also of the whole domain of what should be done: the capacity to receive the exact indication of *how* to do it; and as you go on, it changes into a very clear perception of what must be done, and a precise indication of when it must be done. At least the children, as soon as they have the capacity to think – it starts at the age of seven, but at about fourteen or fifteen it is very clear – the children should be given little indications at the age of seven, a complete explanation at fourteen, of how to do it, and that it is the only way to be in relation with the deeper truth of things, and that all the rest is a more or less clumsy mental approximation to something that can be known directly.

*

When you take the children very young, it is wonderful. There is so little to do: it is enough to *be*.

Never make a mistake.

Never lose your temper.

Always understand.

And to know and see clearly why there has been this movement, why there has been this impulse, what is the inner constitution of the child, what is the thing to be strengthened and brought forward – this is the only thing to do; and to leave them, to leave them free to blossom; simply to give them the opportunity to see many things, to touch many things, to do as many things as possible. It is great fun. And above all, not to try to impose on them what you think you know.

Never scold them. Always understand, and if the child is ready, explain; if he is not ready for an explanation – if you are ready yourself – replace the false vibration by a true one. But this... this is to demand from the teachers a perfection which they rarely have.

But it would be very interesting to make a programme

for the teachers and the true programme of study, from the very bottom – which is so plastic and which receives impressions so deeply. If they were given a few drops of truth when they are very young, they would blossom quite naturally as the being grows. It would be beautiful work.

The Finest Present one can give to a Child

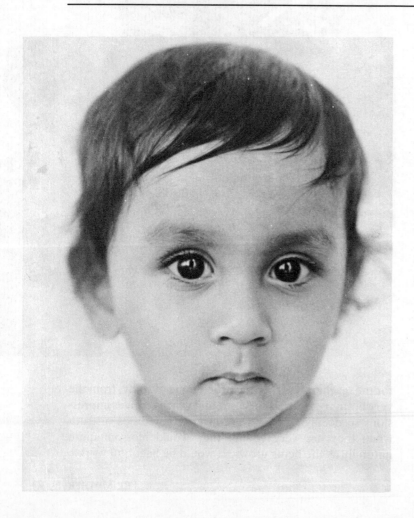

Essentially, the *only thing* you should do assiduously is to teach them to know themselves and choose their own destiny, the path they will follow; to teach them to look at themselves, understand themselves *and* to will what they want to be. That is infinitely more important than teaching them what happened on earth in former times, or even how the earth is built, or even… indeed, all sorts of things which are quite a necessary grounding if you want to live the ordinary life in the world, for if you don't know them, anyone will immediately put you down intellectually: "Oh, he is an idiot, he knows nothing."

But still, at any age, if you are studious and have the will to do it, you can also take up books and work; you don't need to go to school for that. There are enough books in the world to teach you things.

*

It is an invaluable possession for every living being to have learnt to know himself and to master himself. To know oneself means to know the motives of one's actions and reactions, the why and the how of all that happens in oneself. To master oneself means to do what one has decided to do, to do nothing but that, not to listen to or follow impulses, desires or fancies….

The finest present one can give to a child would be to teach him to know himself and to master himself.

To love to learn is the most precious gift that one can make to a child, to learn always and everywhere.

Children must be taught:
a) not to tell a lie, whatever the consequences;
b) to control violence, rage, anger.

If these two things can be done, they can be led towards superhumanity.

There is an idea that if one breaks conventions, restrictions, one is free from the limitations of ordinary humanity. But this is wrong.

Those two things must be achieved to be able to be what may be called "superman": not to tell lies and to control oneself.

A complete devotion to the Divine is the last condition, but these are the first two things to be achieved.

*

The things to be taught to a child
1) The necessity of absolute sincerity.
2) The certitude of the final victory of Truth.
3) The possibility and the will to progress.
Good temper, fair-play, truthfulness.
Patience, endurance, perseverance.
Equanimity, courage, cheerfulness.

*

For the children, precisely because they are children, it would be best to instil in them the will to conquer the future, the will to always look ahead and to want to move on as swiftly as they can towards... what will be – but they should not drag with them the burden, the millstone of the whole oppressive weight of the past. It is only when we are very high in consciousness and knowledge that it is good to look behind to find the points where this future begins to show itself. When we can look at the whole picture, when we have a very global vision, it becomes interesting to know that what will be realised later on has already been announced beforehand, in the same way that Sri Aurobindo said that the divine life will manifest on earth, because it is *already* involved in the depths of Matter; from this standpoint it is interesting to look back or to look down below – not to know what happened, or to know what men have known: that is quite useless.

The children should be told: There are wonderful things to be manifested, prepare yourself to receive them. Then if they want something a little more concrete and easier to understand, you can tell them: Sri Aurobindo came to announce these things; when you are able to read him, you will understand. So this awakens the interest, the desire to learn.

THE MOTHER

Freedom essential for Growth

There are all kinds of different and even opposite theories. Some people say, "Children must be left to have their own experience because it is through experience that they learn things best." Like that, as an idea, it is excellent; in practice it obviously requires some reservations, because if you let a child walk on the edge of a wall and he falls and breaks a leg or his head, the experience is a little hard; or if you let him play with a match-box and he burns out his eyes, you understand, it is paying very dearly for a little knowledge! I have discussed this with... I don't remember now who it was... an educationist, a man concerned with education, who had come from England, and had his ideas about the necessity of an absolute liberty. I made this remark to him; then he said, "But for the love of liberty one can sacrifice the life of many people." It is one opinion.

At the same time, the opposite excess of being there all the time and preventing a child from making his experiment, by telling him, "Don't do this, this will happen", "Don't do that, that will happen" – then finally he will be all shrunk up into himself, and will have neither courage nor boldness in life, and this too is very bad.

In fact it comes to this:

One must never make rules.

Every minute one must endeavour to apply the highest truth one can perceive. It is much more difficult, but it's the only solution.

Whatever you may do, don't make rules beforehand, because once you have made a rule you follow it more or less blindly, and then you are sure, ninety-nine and a half times out of a hundred, to be mistaken.

There is only one way of acting truly, it is to try at each moment, each second, in each movement to express only the highest truth one can perceive, and at the same time know that this perception has to be progressive and that what seems to you the most true now will no longer be so tomorrow, and that a higher truth will have to be expressed more and more through you. This leaves no room any longer for sleeping in a comfortable tamas.

*

I think it was just today or perhaps yesterday, I was pleading for the right of everyone to remain in ignorance if it pleases him – I am not speaking of ignorance from the spiritual point of view, the world of Ignorance in which we live, I am not speaking of that. I am speaking of ignorance according to the classical ideas of education. Well, I say that if there are people who don't want to learn and don't like to learn, they have the right not to learn.

The only thing it is our duty to tell them is this, "Now, you are of an age when your brain is in course of preparation. It is being formed. Each new thing you study makes one more little convolution in your brain. The more you study, the more you think, the more you reflect, the more you work, the more complex and complete does your brain become in its tiny convolutions. And as you are young, it is best done at this time. That is why it is common human practice to choose youth as the period of learning, for it is infinitely easier."...

And so I say: if at about that age some children declare categorically, "Intellectual growth does not interest me at all, I don't want to learn, I want to remain ignorant in the ordinary way of ignorance", I don't see by what right one

could impose studies on them nor why it should be necessary to standardise them.

There are those who are at the bottom and others who are at another level. There are people who may have very remarkable capacities and yet have no taste for intellectual growth. One may warn them that if they don't work, don't study, when they are grown up, they will perhaps feel embarrassed in front of others. But if that does not matter to them and they want to live a non-intellectual life, I believe one has no right to compel them. That is my constant quarrel with the teachers of the school! They come and tell me: "If they don't work, when they are grown up they will be stupid and ignorant." I say: "But if it pleases them to be stupid and ignorant, what right have you to interfere?"

One can't make knowledge and intelligence compulsory. That's all.

WHAT WE SHOULD EXPLAIN TO THE CHILDREN

What is very important is to know what you want. And for this a minimum of freedom is necessary. You must not be under a compulsion or an obligation. You must be able to do things whole-heartedly. If you are lazy, well, you will know what it means to be lazy.... You know, in life idlers are obliged to work ten times more than others, for what they do they do badly, so they are obliged to do it again. But these are things one must learn by experience. They can't be instilled into you.

The mind, if not controlled, is something wavering and imprecise. If one doesn't have the habit of concentrating it upon something, it goes on wandering all the time. It goes on without a stop anywhere and wanders into a *world* of vagueness. And then, when one wants to fix one's attention, it hurts! There is a little effort there, like this: "Oh! how tiring it is, it hurts!" So one does not do it. And one lives in a kind of cloud. And your head is like a cloud; it's like that, most brains are like clouds: there is no precision, no exactitude, no clarity, it is hazy – vague and hazy. You have impressions rather than a knowledge of things. You live in an approximation, and you can keep within you all sorts of contradictory ideas made up mostly of impressions,

sensations, feelings, emotions – all sorts of things like that which have very little to do with thought and... which are just vague ramblings.

But if you want to succeed in having a precise, concrete, clear, definite thought on a certain subject, you must make an effort, gather yourself together, hold yourself firm, concentrate. And the first time you do it, it literally hurts, it is tiring! But if you don't make a habit of it, all your life you will be living in a state of irresolution. And when it comes to practical things, when you are faced with – for, in spite of everything, one is always faced with – a number of problems to solve, of a very practical kind, well, instead of being able to take up the elements of the problem, to put them all face to face, look at the question from every side, and rising above and seeing the solution, instead of that you will be tossed about in the swirls of something grey and uncertain, and it will be like so many spiders running around in your head – but you won't succeed in catching the thing.

I am speaking of the simplest of problems, you know; I am not speaking of deciding the fate of the world or humanity, or even of a country – nothing of the kind. I am speaking of the problems of your daily life, of every day. They become something quite woolly.

Well, it is to avoid this that you are told, when your brain is in course of being formed, "Instead of letting it be shaped by such habits and qualities, try to give it a little exactitude, precision, capacity of concentration, of choosing, deciding, putting things in order, try to use your reason."

Of course, it is well understood that reason is not the supreme capacity of man and must be surpassed, but it is quite obvious that if you don't have it, you will live an altogether incoherent life, you won't even know how to

behave rationally. The least thing will upset you completely and you won't even know why, and still less how to remedy it. While someone who has established within himself a state of active, clear reasoning, can face attacks of all kinds, emotional attacks or any trials whatever; for life is entirely made up of these things – unpleasantness, vexations – which are small but proportionate to the one who feels them, and so naturally felt by him as very big because they are proportionate to him. Well, reason can stand back a little, look at all that, smile and say, "Oh! no, one must not make a fuss over such a small thing."

If you do not have reason, you will be like a cork on a stormy sea. I don't know if the cork suffers from its condition, but it does not seem to me a very happy one.

There, then.

Now, after having said all this – and it's not just once I have told you this but several times I think, and I am ready to tell it to you again as many times as you like – after having said this, I believe in leaving you entirely free to choose whether you want to be the cork on the stormy sea or whether you want to have a clear, precise perception and a sufficient knowledge of things to be able to walk to – well, simply to where you want to go.

For there is a clarity that's indispensable in order to be able even to follow the path one has chosen.

I am not at all keen on your becoming scholars, far from it! For then one falls into the other extreme: one fills one's head with so many things that there is no longer any room for the higher light; but there is a minimum that is indispensable for not... well, for not being the cork.

THE MOTHER

Little Children are Wonderful!

Little children are wonderful. It is quite enough to surround them with things and to let them be. Never interfere unless it is absolutely necessary. And let them be. And never scold them.

*

Up to the age of seven, children should enjoy themselves. School should all be a game, and they learn as they play. As they play they develop a taste for learning, knowing and understanding life. The system is not very important. It is the attitude of the teacher that matters. The teacher should not be something that one endures under constraint. He should always be the friend whom you love because he helps and amuses you.

*

If the children, even very small, are taught to put things in order, classify objects by kind, etc. etc., they like it very much and learn very well. There is a wonderful opportunity to give them good lessons of arrangement and tidiness, *practical, effective lessons*, not theory.

Try and I am sure the children will help you to arrange things.

*

It is obvious that until the child becomes at least a little conscious of itself, it must be subjected to a certain rule, for it has not yet the capacity of choosing for itself.

That age is very variable; it depends on people, depends on each individual. But still, it is understood that in the seven-year period between the age of seven and fourteen, one begins to reach the age of reason. If one is helped, one can become a reasoning being between seven and fourteen.

Before seven there are geniuses – there are always geniuses, everywhere – but as a general rule the child is not conscious of itself and doesn't know why or how to do things. That is the time to cultivate its attention, teach it to concentrate on what it does, give it a small basis sufficient for it not to be entirely like a little animal, but to belong to the human race through an elementary intellectual development.

After that, there is a period of seven years during which it must be taught to choose – to choose what it wants to be. If it chooses to have a rich, complex, well-developed brain, powerful in its functioning, well, it must be taught to work; for it is by work, by reflection, study, analysis and so on that the brain is formed. At fourteen you are ready – or ought to be ready – to know what you want to be.

*

According to what I see and know, as a general rule, children over 14 should be allowed their independence and should be given advice only if and when they ask for it.

They should know that they are responsible for managing their own existence.

*

One must have a lot of patience with young children, and repeat the same thing to them several times, explaining it to them in various ways. It is only gradually that it enters their mind.

*

For children there should be a time for work and study and a time for play.

*

Intelligence and capacity of understanding are surely more important than regularity in work. Steadiness may be acquired later on.

*

The teacher must find out the category to which each of the children in his care belongs. And if after careful observation he discovers two or three exceptional children who are eager to learn and who love progress, he should help them to make use of their energies for this purpose by giving them the freedom of choice that encourages individual growth.

The old method of the seated class to which the teacher gives the same lesson for all, is certainly economical and easy, but also very ineffective, and so time is wasted for everybody.

THE MOTHER

Learning More and Always More

Children have everything to learn. This should be their main preoccupation in order to prepare themselves for a useful and productive life.

At the same time, as they grow up, they must discover in themselves the thing or things which interest them most and which they are capable of doing well. There are latent faculties to be developed. There are also faculties to be discovered.

Children must be taught to like to overcome difficulties, and also that this gives a special value to life; when one knows how to do it, it destroys boredom for ever and gives an altogether new interest to life.

We are on earth to progress and we have everything to learn.

*

Undeniably, what most impedes mental progress in children is the constant dispersion of their thoughts. Their thoughts flutter hither and thither like butterflies and they have to make a great effort to fix them. Yet this capacity is latent in them, for when you succeed in arousing their interest, they are capable of a good deal of attention. By his ingenuity, therefore, the educator will gradually help the child to become capable of a sustained effort of attention and a faculty of more and more complete absorption in the work in hand. All methods that can develop this faculty of attention from games to rewards are good and can all be utilised according to the need and the circumstances. But it is the psychological action that is most important and the sovereign method is to arouse in the child an interest in what you want to teach him, a liking for work, a will to progress. To love to learn is the most precious gift that one can give to a child: to love to learn always and everywhere, so that all circumstances, all happenings in life may be constantly renewed opportunities for learning more and always more.

For that, to attention and concentration should be added observation, precise recording and faithfulness of memory. This faculty of observation can be developed by varied and spontaneous exercises, making use of every opportunity that presents itself to keep the child's thought wakeful, alert and prompt. The growth of the understanding should be stressed much more than that of memory. One knows well only what one has understood. Things learnt by heart, mechanically, fade away little by little and finally disappear; what is understood is never forgotten. Moreover, you must never refuse to explain to a child the how and the why of things. If you cannot do it yourself, you must direct the child to those who are qualified to answer or point out to him some books that deal with the question. In this way you will progressively awaken in the child the taste for true study and the habit of making a persistent effort to know.

This will bring us quite naturally to the second phase of development in which the mind should be widened and enriched.

You will gradually show the child that everything can become an interesting subject for study if it is approached in the right way. The life of every day, of every moment, is the best school of all, varied, complex, full of unexpected experiences, problems to be solved, clear and striking examples and obvious consequences. It is so easy to arouse healthy curiosity in children, if you answer with intelligence and clarity the numerous questions they ask. An interesting reply to one readily brings others in its train and so the attentive child learns without effort much more than he usually does in the classroom. By a choice made with care and insight, you should also teach him to enjoy good reading-matter which is both instructive and attractive. Do not be afraid of anything that awakens and pleases his imagination; imagination develops the creative mental faculty and through it study becomes living and the mind develops in joy.

In order to increase the suppleness and comprehensiveness of his mind, one should see not only that he studies many varied topics, but above all that a single subject is approached in various ways, so that the child understands in a practical manner that there are many ways of facing the same intellectual problem, of considering it and solving it. This will remove all rigidity from his brain and at the same time it will make his thinking richer and more supple and prepare it for a more complex and comprehensive synthesis. In this way also the child will be imbued with the sense of the extreme relativity of mental learning and, little by little, an aspiration for a truer source of knowledge will awaken in him.

*

If, when one was quite young and was taught, for instance, how to squat, if one was taught at the same time not to think or to remain very quiet or to concentrate or gather one's thoughts, or... all sorts of things one must learn to do, like meditating; if, when quite young and at the same time that you were taught to stand straight, for instance, and walk or

sit or even eat – you are taught many things but you are not aware of this, for they are taught when you are very small – if you were taught to meditate also, then spontaneously, later, you could, the day you decide to do so, sit down and meditate. But you are not taught this. You are taught absolutely nothing of the kind. Besides, usually you are taught very few things – you are not taught even to sleep. People think that they have only to lie down in their bed and then they sleep. But this is not true! One must learn how to sleep as one must learn to eat, learn to do anything at all. And if one does not learn, well, one does it badly! Or one takes years and years to learn how to do it, and during all those years when it is badly done, all sorts of unpleasant things occur. And it is only after suffering much, making many mistakes, committing many stupidities, that, gradually, when one is old and has white hair, one begins to know how to do something. But if, when you were quite small, your parents or those who look after you, took the trouble to teach you how to do what you do, do it properly as it should be done, in the right way, then that would help you to avoid all – all these mistakes you make through the years. And not only do you make mistakes, but nobody tells you they are mistakes! And so you are surprised that you fall ill, are tired, don't know how to do what you want to, and that you have never been taught. Some children are not taught anything, and so they need years and years and years to learn the simplest things, even the most elementary thing: to be clean.

It is true that most of the time parents do not teach this because they do not know it themselves! For they themselves did not have anyone to teach them. So they do not know... they have groped in the dark all their life to learn how to live. And so naturally they are not in a position to

teach you how to live, for they do not know it themselves. If you are left to yourself, you understand, it needs years, years of experience to learn the simplest thing, and even then you must think about it. If you don't think about it, you will never learn.

To live in the right way is a very difficult art, and unless one begins to learn it when quite young and to make an effort, one never knows it very well. Simply the art of keeping one's body in good health, one's mind quiet and goodwill in one's heart – things which are indispensable in order to live decently – I don't say in comfort, I don't say remarkably, I only say decently. Well, I don't think there are many who take care to teach this to their children.

*

All studies, or in any case the greater part of studies consists in learning about the past, in the hope that it will give you a better understanding of the present. But if you want to avoid the danger that the students may cling to the past and refuse to look to the future, you must take great care to explain to them that the purpose of everything that

happened in the past was to prepare what is taking place now, and that everything that is taking place now is nothing but a preparation for the road towards the future, which is truly the most important thing for which we must prepare.

It is by cultivating intuition that one prepares to live for the future.

*

Everyone should be taught the joy of doing well whatever he does, whether it is intellectual, artistic or manual work, and above all, the dignity of all work, whatever it may be, when it is done with care and skill.

*

I insist on the necessity of having good manners. I do not see anything grand in the manners of a gutter-snipe.

*

In unformed minds what they read sinks in without any regard to its value and imprints itself as truth. It is advisable therefore to be careful about what one gives them to read and to see that only what is true and useful for their formation gets a place.

*

It is not so much a question of subject-matter but of vulgarity of mind and narrowness and selfish common-sense in the conception of life, expressed in a form devoid of art, greatness or refinement, which must be carefully removed from the reading-matter of children both big and small. All that lowers and degrades the consciousness must be excluded.

THE MOTHER

Never to Scold

A child should never be scolded. I am accused of speaking ill of parents! but I have seen them at work, you see, and I know that ninety per cent of parents snub a child who comes spontaneously to confess a mistake: "You are very naughty. Go away, I am busy" – instead of listening to the child with patience and explaining to him where his fault lies, how he ought to have acted. And the child, who had come with good intentions, goes away quite hurt, with the feeling: "Why am I treated thus?" Then the child sees his parents are not perfect – which is obviously true of them today – he sees that they are wrong and says to himself: "Why does he scold me, he is like me!"

*

Another pitfall to avoid: do not scold your child without good reason and only when it is quite indispensable. A child who is too often scolded gets hardened to rebuke and no longer attaches much importance to words or severity of tone. And above all, take good care never to scold him for a fault which you yourself commit. Children are very keen and clear-sighted observers; they soon find out your weaknesses and note them without pity.

When a child has done something wrong, see that he confesses it to you spontaneously and frankly; and when he has confessed, with kindness and affection make him understand what was wrong in his movement so that he will not repeat it, but never scold him; a fault confessed must always be forgiven. You should not allow any fear to come between you and your child; fear is a pernicious means of

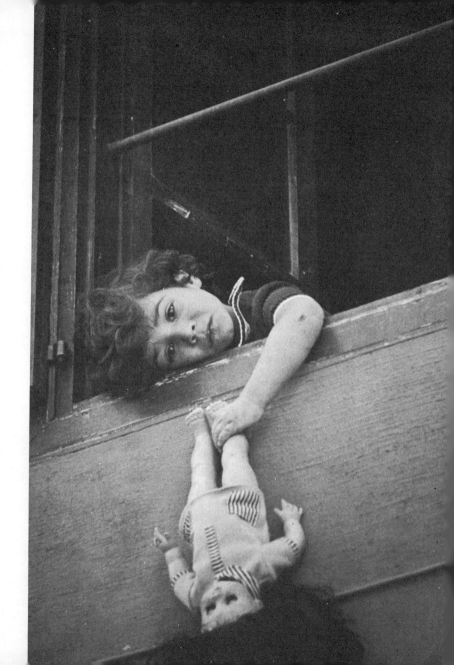

education: it invariably gives birth to deceit and lying. Only a discerning affection that is firm yet gentle and an adequate practical knowledge will create the bonds of trust that are indispensable for you to be able to educate your child effectively. And do not forget that you have to control yourself constantly in order to be equal to your task and truly fulfil the duty which you owe your child by the mere fact of having brought him into the world.

*

A child ought to stop being naughty because he learns to be ashamed of being naughty, not because he is afraid of punishment.

In the first case, he makes true progress.

In the second, he falls one step down in human consciousness, for fear is a degradation of consciousness.

*

To hit the children – all blows are forbidden, even the slightest little slap or the so-called friendly punch. To give a blow to a child because he does not obey or does not understand or because he is disturbing the others indicates a lack of self-control, and it is harmful for both teacher and student.

Disciplinary measures may be taken if necessary, but in complete calm and not because of a personal reaction.

*

You are a good teacher but it is your way of dealing with the children that is objectionable.

The children must be educated in an atmosphere of love and gentleness.

No violence, never.

No scolding, never.

Always a gentle kindness and the teacher must be the *living example* of the virtues the child must acquire.

The children must be *happy* to go to school, *happy* to learn, and the teacher must be their best friend who gives them the example of the qualities they must acquire.

And all that depends exclusively on the teacher. What he does and how he behaves.

*

Q: Sweet Mother, should one punish a child?

Punish? What do you mean by punish? If a child is noisy in class and prevents the others from working, you must tell him to behave himself; and if he continues, you can send him out of the class. That is not a punishment, it is a natural consequence of his actions. But to punish! To punish! You have no right to punish. Are you the Divine? Who has given you the right to punish? The children too can punish you for your actions. Are you perfect yourselves? Do you know what is good or what is bad? Only the Divine knows. Only the Divine has the right to punish.

The vibrations that you emit bring you into contact with corresponding vibrations. If you emit harmful and destructive vibrations, quite naturally you draw corresponding vibrations towards yourselves and that is the real punishment, if you want to use that word; but it does not correspond at all to the divine organisation of the world.

THE MOTHER

To Find the Inner Truth

There is another quality which must be cultivated in a child from a very young age: that is the feeling of uneasiness, of a moral disbalance which it feels when it has done certain things, not because it has been told not to do them, not because it fears punishment, but spontaneously. For example, a child who hurts its comrade through mischief, if it is in its normal, natural state, will experience uneasiness, a grief deep in its being, because what it has done is contrary to its inner truth.

For in spite of all teachings, in spite of all that thought can think, there is something in the depths which has a feeling of a perfection, a greatness, a truth, and is painfully contradicted by all the movements opposing this truth. If a child has not been spoilt by its milieu, by deplorable examples around it, that is, if it is in the normal state, spontaneously, without its being told anything, it will feel an uneasiness when it has done something against the truth of its being. And it is exactly upon this that later its effort for progress must be founded.

For, if you want to find one teaching, one doctrine upon which to base your progress, you will never find anything – or, to be more exact, you will find something else, for in accordance with the climate, the age, the civilisation, the teaching given is quite conflicting. When one person says, "This is good", another will say, "No, this is bad", and with the same logic, the same persuasive force. Consequently, it is not upon this that one can build. Religion has always tried to establish a dogma, and it will tell you that if you conform to the dogma you are in the truth and if you don't you are in the falsehood. But all this has never led to

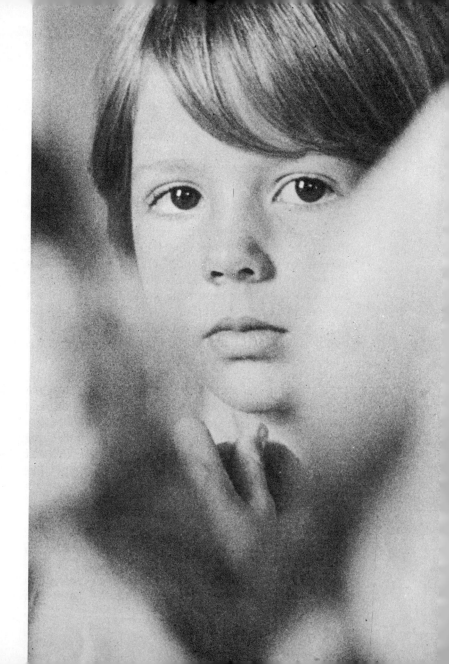

anything and has only created confusion.

There is only one true guide, that is the inner guide, who does not pass through the mental consciousness.

Naturally, if a child gets a disastrous education, it will try ever harder to extinguish within itself this little true thing, and sometimes it succeeds so well that it loses all contact with it, and also the power of distinguishing between good and evil. That is why I insist upon this, and I say that from their infancy children must be taught that there is an inner reality – within themselves, within the earth, within the universe – and that they, the earth and the universe exist only as a function of this truth, and that if it did not exist the child would not last, even the short time that it does, and that everything would dissolve even as it comes into being. And because this is the real basis of the universe, naturally it is this which will triumph; and all that opposes this cannot endure as long as this does, because it is That, the eternal thing which is at the base of the universe.

It is not a question, of course, of giving a child philosophical explanations, but he could very well be given the feeling of this kind of inner comfort, of satisfaction, and sometimes, of an intense joy when he obeys this little very silent thing within him which will prevent him from doing what is contrary to it. It is on an experience of this kind that teaching may be based. The child must be given the impression that nothing can endure if he does not have within himself this true satisfaction which alone is permanent.

*

Q: Can a child become conscious of this inner truth like an adult?

For a child this is very clear, for it is a perception without any complications of word or thought – there is that which puts him at ease and that which makes him uneasy (it is not necessarily joy or sorrow which come only when the thing is very intense). And all this is much clearer in the child than in an adult, for the latter has always a mind which works and clouds his perception of the truth.

To give a child theories is absolutely useless, for as soon as his mind awakes he will find a thousand reasons for contradicting your theories, and he will be right.

This little true thing in the child is the divine Presence in the psychic – it is also there in plants and animals. In plants it is not conscious, in animals it begins to be conscious, and in children it is very conscious. I have known children who were much more conscious of their psychic being at the age of five than at fourteen, and at fourteen than at twenty-five; and above all, from the moment they go to school where they undergo that kind of intensive mental training which draws their attention to the intellectual part of their being, they lose almost always and almost completely this contact with their psychic being.

If only you were an experienced observer, if you could tell what goes on in a person, simply by looking into his eyes!... It is said the eyes are the mirror of the soul; that is a popular way of speaking but if the eyes do not express to you the psychic, it is because it is very far behind, veiled by many things. Look carefully, then, into the eyes of little children, and you will see a kind of light – some describe it as frank – but so true, so true, which looks at the world with wonder. Well, this sense of wonder, it is the wonder of the psychic which sees the truth but does not understand much about the world, for it is too far from it. Children have this but as they learn more, become more intelligent, more educated, this is effaced, and you see all sorts of things in their eyes: thoughts, desires, passions, wickedness – but

this kind of little flame, so pure, is no longer there. And you may be sure it is the mind that has got in there, and the psychic has gone very far behind.

Even a child who does not have a sufficiently developed brain to understand, if you simply pass on to him a vibration of protection or affection or solicitude or consolation, you will see that he responds. But if you take a boy of fourteen, for example, who is at school, who has ordinary parents and has been ill-treated, his mind is very much in the forefront; there is something hard in him, the psychic being has gone behind. Such boys do not respond to the vibration. One would say they are made of wood or plaster.

*

It is quite evident that all evil – at least what we call evil – all falsehood, all that is contrary to the Truth, all suffering, all opposition is the result of a disequilibrium. I believe that one who is habituated to seeing things from this higher plane sees immediately that it is like that. Consequently, the world cannot be founded upon a disequilibrium, for if so it would have long since disappeared. One feels that at the origin of the universe there must have been a supreme Equilibrium and, perhaps, as we said the other day, a progressive equilibrium, an equilibrium which is the exact opposite of all that we have been taught and all that we are accustomed to call "evil". There is no absolute evil, but *an* evil, a more or less partial disequilibrium.

This may be taught to a child in a very simple way; it may be shown with the help of material things that an object will fall if it is not balanced, that only things in equilibrium can keep their position and duration.

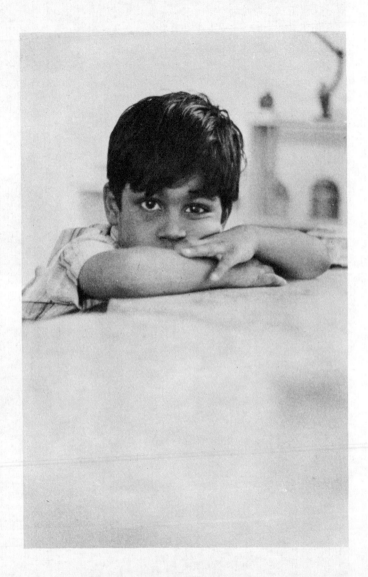

THE MOTHER

When Children Cry for Things

Q: Sweet Mother, why do some children have the habit of always asking for things? Material things, like sweets, everything they see...

Oh, because they are full of desires. They were probably formed with vibrations of desires, and as they have no control over themselves it is expressed freely. Older people are also full of desires, but usually they have a kind of... how do we call it?... They are a little shy of showing their desires or they feel a bit ashamed or perhaps are afraid they will be laughed at; so they don't show them. Well, they too are full of desires. Only children are more simple. When they want something they say so. They don't tell themselves that perhaps it would be wiser not to show this, because they don't yet have this kind of reasoning. But I think, generally speaking, with very few exceptions, that people live in perpetual desires. Only, they don't express them, and sometimes they are ashamed also to acknowledge it to themselves. But it is there, this need of having something... you know, one sees something pretty, it is immediately translated into a desire for possession; and this is one of the things... it is absolutely childish. It is childish and indeed it is ridiculous, because at least ninety times out of a hundred, when the one who had a desire for something possesses it, he doesn't even look at it any longer. It is very rarely that this thing continues to interest him once he has it, whatever the nature of the object.

*

Q: Sweet Mother, how can we help a child to come out of this habit of always asking?

There are many ways. But first of all you must know whether you will not just stop him from freely expressing what he thinks and feels. Because this is what people usually do. They scold, even sometimes punish him; and so the child forms the habit of concealing his desires. But he is not cured of them. And you see, if he is always told, "No, you won't have that", then, simply, this state of mind gets settled in him: "Ah, when you are small, people don't give you anything! You must wait till you are big. When I am big I shall have all that I want." That's how it is. But this does not cure them. It is very difficult to bring up a child. There is a way which consists in giving him all he wants; and naturally, the next minute he will want something else, because that's the law, the law of desire: never to be satisfied. And so, if he is intelligent, one can tell him, "But you see, you insisted so much on having this and now you longer care for it. You want something else." Yet if he was very clever he would answer, "Well, the best way of curing me is to give me what I ask for."

Some people cherish this idea all their life. When they are told that they should overcome their desires, they say, "The easiest way is to satisfy them." This kind of logic seems impeccable. But the fact is that it is not the object desired that has to be changed, it is the impulse of desire, the movement of desire. And for this a great deal of knowledge is needed, and this is difficult for a very young child.

It is difficult. Indeed, they don't have the capacity for

reasoning; one can't explain things to them, because they don't understand the reasons. So you see, when it is like that the parents usually tell the child, "Keep quiet, you are a nuisance!" In this way they get out of the difficulty. But this is no solution. It is very difficult. It asks for a sustained effort and an unshakable patience. Some people are like that all their life; they are like babies throughout their existence and it is impossible to make them see reason. As soon as one tells them that they are not reasonable and that one can't all the time be giving them things to satisfy their desires, they simply think, "These people are unpleasant. This person is not nice." That's all.

In fact, perhaps one should begin by shifting the movement to things which it is better to have from the true point of view, and which it is more difficult to obtain. If one could turn this impulsion of desire towards a... For example, when a child is full of desires, if one could give him a desire of a higher kind – instead of its being a desire for purely material objects, you understand, an altogether transitory satisfaction – if one could awaken in him the desire to know, the desire to learn, the desire to become a remarkable person... in this way, begin with that. As these things are difficult to do, so, gradually, he will develop his will for these things. Or even, from the material point of view, the desire to do something difficult, as for example, construct a toy which it is difficult to make – or give him a game of patience which requires a great deal of perseverance.

If one can orient them – it requires much discernment, much patience, but it can be done – and if one can orient them towards something like this, to succeed in very difficult games or to work out something which requires much care and attention, and can push them in some line like this so that it exercises a persevering will in them, then this can have results: turn their attention away from certain things and towards others. This needs constant care and it seems to be a way that's most – I can't say the easiest, for it is certainly not easy – but the most effective way. To say "No" does not cure and to say "Yes" does not cure either; and sometimes it becomes extremely difficult also, naturally.

I knew people, for example, whose children wanted to eat everything they saw. They were allowed to do it. So they fell very ill. After that, they felt disgusted. But this is a little risky, isn't it? There are children who fidget with everything. Now, one day, you see, one child got hold of a box of matches. Then, instead of telling him, "Don't touch it", they let him do it: he burnt himself. He never touched them again.

But it is a little dangerous, because some children are altogether unconscious and very bold in their desires: for example, those who like to walk on the edge of a wall or the top of a roof or have the desire to plunge into water when they see it or to dive into a river... you see, this becomes sometimes very difficult... or those who have the mania for crossing the street: each time they see a car coming... they try to cross it. So if they are allowed to do so, the experience may one day be fatal...

Probably, one needs to find a middle term between the two, between the two extremes: that of watching over him all the time and that of leaving him absolutely free to do what he likes, without even warning him against the accidents which are likely to occur. An adjustment to make every minute! Difficult.

THE MOTHER

44

When Children Play with Swords and Pistols

Q: Because all the tendencies of the children come into play when they are given enough free scope, several difficulties arise, especially in controlling the noise and movements they make. A few days ago, they began to make swords and pistols out of meccano. So, in a general way, when these things come up, when the children are engaged in this kind of activity, should we intervene, or wait until the movement dies down and disappears?

You should... you should question the children and ask them in an off-hand way, "Oh, you have enemies? Who are these enemies?"... That is what you should say.... You should make them talk a little.... It is because they see that... There is a strength and a beauty in the army which children feel strongly. But that should be preserved. Only, armies should be used not to attack and capture but to defend and... protect.

First you must understand properly: for the moment,

we are in a condition where weapons are still necessary. We have to understand that this is a passing condition, not final, but that we must move towards that.

Peace – peace, harmony – should be the natural result of a change of consciousness....

You see, there is this idea of non-violence about India, which has replaced material violence by moral violence – but that is far worse!

You should make them understand this.... You can say this, explain to the children that to replace physical violence, material violence, by moral violence, is no better.

Lying down in front of a train to prevent it from passing is a moral violence which can create more disturbances than physical violence. You... can you hear me?

But it depends on the child, it depends on the case. You must not give any names, say what this or that person has said. We must make them understand ideas and reactions.

You should... That is a good example: you should make them understand that lying down in front of a train to prevent it from passing is as great a violence... even greater than attacking it with weapons. You understand, there are many, many things that could be said. It depends on the case.

I myself encouraged fencing a great deal because it gives a skill, a control of one's movements and a discipline in violence. At one time I encouraged fencing a great deal, and then too, I learned to shoot. I used to shoot with a pistol, I used to shoot with a rifle because that gives you a steadiness and skill and a sure-sightedness that is excellent, and it obliges you to stay calm in the midst of danger. I don't see why all these things... One must not be hopelessly non-violent – that makes characters that are... soft!

You should have taken the opportunity to tell them, "Oh, you should learn fencing!"

And a pistol too?

Q: Yes, Mother.

And tell them... teach them to shoot... make it into an *art*, into an art and into a training of calm and self-controlled skill. One should never... never raise hue and cry.... That will not do at all, at all, at all. I am not at all in favour of that. The methods of self-defence should be mastered, and for that they must be practised.

THE MOTHER

Some Reminiscences

Here are a few anecdotes collected from the reminiscences of those who had the privilege of being close to the Mother and seeing her with children. The anecdotes reveal not only the Mother's deep love for them but also her unique way of looking at a situation so that nothing remains trivial and all is suffused with a deeper significance.

THE TRUE VALUE OF A PERSON

I was helping to look after one of the first boardings which was started by the Mother. One day, during dinner, one of the boys proclaimed very proudly that his father always travelled in style, only 'first class.' I told the Mother about this the following day. The Mother asked me what had been my response. I replied that I had simply ignored it. But she said that I ought not to have done that and added that, when the opportunity arose, I should call the children together and explain to them that worldly wealth is of no importance; only the wealth that has been offered to the Divine has a value. You do not become big by living in big houses, travelling by first class and spending money lavishly. You increase in stature only by being truthful, sincere, obedient, grateful and by serving the Divine.

THE IMPORTANCE OF WORK

Once some coconuts were being distributed in the Ashram. The mother of a young girl had not come. But when the girl was asked to carry it, she refused saying that she felt shy to carry a coconut on the road. When I informed the Mother of this incident she said that all children should be encouraged to take up some work as part of their education so that they could overcome such reactions and realise the true value of work. I was asked to organise immediately this activity. It evoked an enthusiastic response from the children, specially when they realised how happy the Mother was to see them work.

EDUCATION CANNOT BE SOLD

Once the Ashram was in a tight financial situation. Some disciples pointed out that we were giving free education to so many children and spending large sums of money on them. Many of the children were from well-to-do families and no one would mind if we fixed a nominal fee for the education provided. On the other hand, it would help the Ashram considerably. The Mother replied in a serious tone that in India education had never been sold and she would not do it. The question was never raised again.

SOME HINTS FOR THE PARENTS

I was looking after some children in a boarding and the Mother always took interest in all the aspects of the children's lives. On different occasions she told us the following:

a) To wake a sleeping child, one should not call him loudly by his name or touch his body. Instead, one should gently and softly call him.

b) It is very important to teach the children to sleep and eat at a fixed time. While eating, the children should be encouraged to feel what are the needs of the body rather than to be led by taste. If some children like to over-eat they need not be refused but they should be given a smaller helping from the beginning.

c) Nothing should be imposed on the children. They may be made to do what one will by explaining to them in the proper way, but never by compulsion.

THE NEWSPAPER AND THE SWEETS

During the early days of my association with the Mother, I once took to Her a big basket of sweets from Delhi for my children.

The Mother opened the basket and saw that the sweets were wrapped in newspaper. She, immediately called someone standing close to Her, handed over the basket and asked him to throw it away.

She said, "You see, the sweets packed in newspapers cannot be given to children for eating. The inks with which the newspapers are printed are poisonous. And newspapers are always dirty."

I realised how particular the Mother was with things concerning the children. I also felt that when my children were bathed in the Mother's love and sweetness where was the need of sweets from Delhi.

THE MOTHER — HUMAN AND DIVINE

My child P. had been admitted to the children's boarding in the Ashram.

One morning I was going home from the Ashram and P. was following me on the road. I heard a loud scream. I turned and saw that he had fallen and hurt himself. There

was a deep cut on his forehead. His clothes, were blood-stained.

I ran to lift him up and take him home but before I could do that he had got up crying and instead of coming towards me started running in the opposite direction. I was surprised. I ran after him, I called him several times, but he would not hear and went back into the Ashram. I kept calling him but he would not hear and ran even faster.

I had also to run after him. He went straight up the staircase and reached the Mother. I was astonished that instead of coming to me he ran back that distance to reach the Mother.

The Mother held him and asked, "Mon Petit, what happened?" He was hardly three and so he could not converse with the Mother either in English or in French. He just fell down again on the floor before the Mother, gesturing that this is what had happened. Although he was still bleeding he had stopped crying now because he wanted to explain to the Mother exactly what had happened.

Mother went in and brought Her First Aid box, washed his forehead with spirit, bandaged it nicely and showered him with love. She also gave him some 'Sweets' and sent him home with me.

I was amazed to see the beauty of Divine Love becoming human.

GAMES OF SKILL

The Mother was very fond of games of skill. She once told me that we should introduce games where fine skill was required. To show us the importance of developing this skill she asked each of us in turn to lift the cover of a crystal bowl and replace it without making the slightest sound. We

all tried, but it was Mother who replaced it without the least sound.

I told Mother that we had already introduced some games of skill for children, at the Library of Physical Education. She seemed pleased to hear it.

Whenever people brought Her games of skill, She would give them to us. We soon had a little corner all to ourselves where we kept all these games. We played "fiddlestix", "flying hats", etc. but most of all we played "Jonches", a Japanese game which was Mother's favourite.

Jonches was played with fine match-like sticks. These were either collected together in the hand, and released all together, or to make the game more difficult, they were arranged one on top of the other. Each player in turn had to pick up as many sticks as he could without moving any other stick. If any stick, other than the one being lifted moved, the player lost his turn. The one with the maximum number of sticks was the winner.

Mother was so fond of this game, that She would come and join us whenever She could spare a little time. She would sit down on the carpet and play with us. Later, a little table was provided for us and when Mother came to play, there was a small stool for Her to sit on.

HELPING THE MOTHER IN YOGA

In the fifties the Mother took French classes for the children. During one of these Friday evening classes in the Playground one of the children asked the Mother: "What can we do to help you, Mother, in the Yoga?" There was general laughter. But Mother was quite serious, and after some time She said very simply:

"Be happy."

Again there was laughter and the child said: "But Mother we are always happy." The Mother continued, "Yes, that is good because when you are happy here it means you are on the right path – but immediately you feel uneasy or not so happy, it means there is something wrong which you have to attend to – something wrong with you which you have to correct."

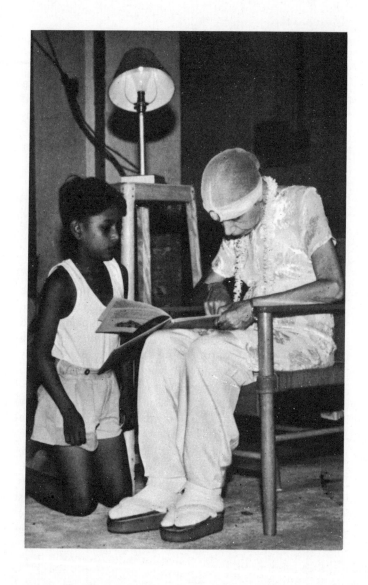

Thou Art That

When Svetaketu was twelve years old, his father Uddalaka said to him, "Svetaketu, you must now go to school and study. None of our family, my child, is ignorant of Brahman."

Thereupon Svetaketu went to a teacher and studied for twelve years. After committing to memory all the Vedas, he returned home full of pride in his learning.

His father, noticing the young man's conceit, said to him: "Svetaketu, have you asked for that knowledge by which we hear the unhearable, by which we perceive the unperceivable, by which we know the unknowable?"

"What is that knowledge, sir?" asked Svetaketu.

"My child, as by knowing one lump of clay, all things made of clay are known, the difference being only in name and arising from speech, and the truth being that all are clay; as by knowing a nugget of gold, all things made of gold are known, the difference being only in name and arising from speech, and the truth being that all are gold – exactly so is that knowledge, knowing which we know all."

"But surely those venerable teachers of mine are ignorant of this knowledge; for if they had possessed it, they would have taught it to me. Do you therefore, sir, give me that knowledge."

"Be it so," said Uddalaka, and continued thus:

"In the beginning there was Existence, One only, without a second. Some say that in the beginning there was non-existence only, and that out of that the universe was born. But how could such a thing be? How could existence be born of non-existence? No, my son, in the beginning there was Existence alone – One only, without a second.

He, the One thought to himself: Let me be many, let me grow forth. Thus out of himself he projected the universe; and having projected out of himself the universe, he entered into every being. All that is has its self in him alone. Of all things he is the subtle essence. He is the truth. He is the Self. And that, Svetaketu, THAT ART THOU."

"Please, sir, tell me more about this Self."

"Be it so, my child:

"As the bees make honey by gathering juices from many flowering plants and trees, and as these juices reduced to one honey do not know from what flowers they severally come, similarly, my son, all creatures, when they are merged in that one Existence, whether in dreamless sleep or in death, know nothing of their past or present state, because of the ignorance enveloping them – know

not that they are merged in him and that from him they came.

"Whatever these creatures are, whether a lion, or a tiger, or a boar, or a worm, or a gnat, or a mosquito, that they remain after they come back from dreamless sleep.

"All these have their self in him alone. He is the truth. He is the subtle essence of all. He is the Self. And that, Svetaketu, THAT ART THOU."

"Please, sir, tell me more about this Self."

"Be it so, my son:

"The rivers in the east flow eastward, the rivers in the west flow westward, and all enter into the sea. From sea to sea they pass, the clouds lifting them to the sky as vapour and sending them down as rain. And as these rivers, when they are united with the sea, do not know whether they are this or that river, likewise all those creatures that I have named, when they come back from Brahman, know not whence they came.

"All those beings have their self in him alone. He is the truth. He is the subtle essence of all. He is the Self. And that, Svetaketu, THAT ART THOU."

"Please, sir, tell me more about this Self."

"Be it so, my child:

"If someone were to strike once at the root of this large tree, it would bleed, but live. If he were to strike at its stem, it would bleed, but live. If he were to strike at the top, it would bleed, but live. Pervaded by the living Self, this tree stands firm, and takes its food; but if the Self were to depart from one of its branches, that branch would wither; if it were to depart from a second, that would wither; if it were to depart from a third, that would wither. If it were to depart from the whole tree, the whole tree would wither.

"Likewise, my son, know this: The body dies when the

Self leaves it – but the Self dies not.

"All that is, has its self in him alone. He is the truth. He is the subtle essence of all. He is the Self. And that, Svetaketu, THAT ART THOU."

"Please, sir, tell me more about this Self."

"Be it so. Bring a fruit of that Nyagrodha tree."

"Here it is, sir."

"Break it."

"It is broken, sir."

"What do you see?"

"Some seeds, extremely small, sir."

"Break one of them."

"It is broken, sir."

"What do you see?"

"Nothing, sir."

"The subtle essence you do not see, and in that is the whole of the Nyagrodha tree. Believe, my son, that that which is the subtle essence – in that have all things their existence. That is the truth. That is the Self. And that, Svetaketu, THAT ART THOU."

"Please, sir, tell me more about this Self."

"Be it so. Put this salt in water, and come to me tomorrow morning."

Svetaketu did as he was bidden. The next morning his father asked him to bring the salt which he had put in the water. But he could not, for it had dissolved. Then said Uddalaka:

"Sip the water, and tell me how it tastes."

"It is salty, sir."

"In the same way," continued Uddalaka, "though you do not see Brahman in this body, he is indeed here. That which is the subtle essence – in that have all things their existence. That is the truth. That is the Self. And that, Svetaketu, THAT ART THOU."

"Please, sir, tell me more about this Self," said the youth again.

"Be it so, my child:

"As a man may be blindfolded, and led away, and left in a strange place; and as, having been so dealt with, he turns in every direction and cries out for someone to remove his bandages and show him the way home; and as one thus entreated may loose his bandages and give him comfort; and as thereupon he walks from village to village, asking his way as he goes; and as he arrives home at last – just so does a man who meets with an illumined teacher obtain true knowledge.

"That which is the subtle essence – in that have all beings their existence. That is the truth. That is the Self. And that, O Svetaketu, THAT ART THOU."

"Please, sir, tell me more about this Self."

54   "Be it so, my child:

"When a man is fatally ill, his relations gather round him and ask, 'Do you know me? Do you know me?' Now until his speech is merged in his mind, his mind in his breath, his breath in his vital heat, his vital heat in the Supreme Being, he knows them. But when his speech is merged in his mind, his mind in his breath, his breath in his vital heat, his vital heat in the Supreme Being, then he does not know them.

"That which is the subtle essence – in that have all beings their existence. That is the truth. That is the Self. And that, O Svetaketu, THAT ART THOU."

Father Flanagan's Toughest Customer

By Fulton Oursler

"There's no such thing as a bad boy!" – and then along came Eddie...

One winter night a long-distance call came to that Nebraska village known all over the world as Boys Town.

"Father Flanagan? This is Sheriff Hosey – from Virginia. Got room for another boy – immediately?"

"Where is he now?"

"In jail. He's a desperate character – robbed a bank, held up three stores with a revolver."

"How old is he?"

"Eight and a half."

The gaunt, blue-eyed priest stiffened at the telephone. *"He's what?"*

"Don't let his age fool you. He's all I said he was, and more. Will you take him off our hands?"

For years the Rev. Edward Joseph Flanagan has been taking unwanted boys off the hands of baffled society: youths of all ages, races, creeds.

"If I can't manage an eight-year-old by this time, I ought to quit," he said. "Bring him on!"

Three days later, Sheriff Hosey and his wife set down their prisoner in Father Flanagan's office – an unnaturally pale boy with a bundle under his arm. He was no higher than the desk; frowzy hair of chocolate brown dangled over the pinched face; sullen brown eyes were half shut beneath long, dark lashes. From one side of his mouth a cigarette drooped at a theatrical angle. "Don't mind the smoking," pleaded the sheriff. "We had to bribe him with cigarettes."

The sheriff's wife laid a long envelope on the desk.

"There's a complete report," she snapped. "And that's not the half of it. This good-for-nothing criminal is not worth helping. It's my personal opinion he ain't even human! Good-bye and good luck – you're going to need it!"

Now the heart of Father Flanagan is warmed by his love of God and man, and especially young ones. Looking upon this patched wraith of childhood, the priest thought that never had he seen such a mixture of the comical and the utterly squalid and tragic.

Waving the newcomer to a chair, Father Flanagan began to read the report. People had forgotten the boy's last name; he was just Eddie. Born in a slum near the Newport News docks, he had lost mother and father in a flu epidemic before he was four. In water-front flats he was shunted from one family to another, living like a desperate animal.

Hardship sharpened his cunning and his will. At the age of eight he became the boss of a gang of boys, some nearly twice his age. Coached by older toughs of the neighborhood, Eddie browbeat them into petty crimes which he planned in detail.

About six months before the law caught up with him, his rule had been challenged by a new member of the gang.

"You never do anything yourself. You're no leader."

"I'll show you," replied Eddie. "I'll do something you wouldn't dare. I'm going to rob a bank."

The bank was housed in an old-fashioned building. When most of the clerks were at lunch, Eddie entered unseen and crossed to an unattended slot of the cashier cage. So small that he had to chin himself up, he thrust in one grimy paw, seized a packet of bills and hid them in his jacket. Then he walked out to divide $ 200 among his comrades. But the exploit was a flop; the bank concealed the theft and there were no headlines.

"You're only cracking your jaw," the gang jeered. "You found that dough somewhere."

Eddie's answer was to disappear for several days. Someone had sold him a revolver, and he was out in the fields beyond town, practising marksmanship.

This time the local front pages were full of him. Slouching into a restaurant at a quiet hour, he aimed his gun at the terrified counterman and was handed the day's take from the cash register. Next he dragged a roll of bills from the pocket of a quaking tailor. His third call was on an old lady who kept a candy store.

"Put that thing down," this grandmother cried, "before you hurt yourself!"

She smacked the gun out of his hand and grabbed him by the hair. Savagely he struggled; he might have killed her, but her screams brought policemen. Now Eddie had wound up in Boys Town.

Putting aside the report, Father Flanagan looked at the villain of the piece. In the dimmish light Eddie sat unmoving, head lowered, so that it was hard to see much of that sullen face. As the man watched, the child produced a cigarette paper and a sack of tobacco. One hand, cowboy fashion, he deliberately rolled a cigarette and lit it, thumb-

nail to match; he blew a plume of smoke across the desk.

The long eyelashes lifted for a flash, to see how the priest was taking it.

"Eddie," began Flanagan, "you are welcome here. The whole place is run by the fellows, you know. Boy mayor. Boy city council. Boy chief of police."

"Where's the jail?" grunted Eddie.

"We haven't a jail. You are going to take a bath and then get supper. Tomorrow you start in a school. You and I can become real friends – it's strictly up to you. Some day I hope I can take you to my heart. I know you're a good boy!"

The reply came in one shocking syllable.

About ten o'clock next morning Father Flanagan's office door opened and the new pupil swaggered in. His hair had been cut and neatly combed and he was clean. With an air of great unconcern he tossed on the desk a note from one of the teachers: "Dear Father Flanagan: We have heard you say a thousand times that there is no such thing as a bad boy. Would you mind telling me what you call this one?"

Back in the classroom Father Flanagan found the atmosphere tense. The teacher described how Eddie had sat quietly in his seat for about an hour; suddenly he began parading up and down the aisle, swearing like a longshoreman and throwing movable objects on the floor, finally pitching an inkwell which landed accurately on a plaster bust of Cicero.

Replacing Eddie in his seat, Father Flanagan apologized:

"It was my fault. I never told him he mustn't throw inkwells. The laws of Boys Town will, of course, be enforced withhim, as with all the rest of us. But he has to learn them first. We must never forget that Eddie is a good boy."

"Like hell I am!" screamed Eddie.

The child made no friends among boys or teachers. And for Father Flanagan he reserved his supreme insult – "a damned praying Christian." Spare time he spent roaming about stealthily, looking for a chance to run away. He stood aloof in the gymnasium and on baseball and football fields: "Kid stuff!" he muttered. Neither choir nor band could stir him; the farm bored him. And in all that first six months not once a laugh or a tear. Soon the question in Boys Town was whether Father Flanagan had met his match at last.

"Does the little fellow learn anything?" he asked the sisters.

"Somehow he is getting his A B C's," they reported. "In fact he's learning more than he lets on. But he's just eaten up with hate."

This was not the first tough case Father Flanagan had dealt with. One youngster had shot his father, a wifebeater, through the heart. A murderer – but only because the lad loved his mother. When the priest had understood, he had been able to work things out. There must be something in Eddie, too, that could be worked out.

"I'll have to throw away the book of rules," grumbled Flanagan. "I'm going to try spoiling the little devil – with love!"

Boys and teachers watched the new strategy as if it were a sporting contest, and the home team was Father Flanagan. Upon those weeks and months of planned treats the priest looks back with a reminiscent shudder: the scores of second-rate movies they sat through; the hot dogs and hamburgers, candy bars, ice cream and soft drinks that Eddie stuffed inside his puny body.

Yet never once did Eddie give a sign that anything was

fun. In summer dawns that smelled of pines and wild clover, he would trudge stolidly down to the lake, but no grunt of excitement came when he landed a trout. An apathy settled upon him; he became more silent than ever.

Only once toward the end of that unhappy experiment did man and boy come closer together. At a street crossing in Omaha Eddie was looking in the wrong direction when a truck bore down on him; Father Flanagan yanked him out of harm's way. For one instant a light of gratitude flickered in the startled brown eyes, then the dark lashes fell again; he said nothing.

Even to the man of faith it began to seem that here was an inherent vileness beyond his reach. Hope had fallen to the lowest possible point when one soft spring morning Eddie appeared in the office, boldly announcing that he wanted to have it out with Father Flanagan. This time the brown eyes were glowing with indignation.

"You been trying to get around me," he began, "but now I'm wise to you. If you was on the level, I might have been a sucker, at that. I almost fell for your line. But last night I got to thinking it over and I see the joker in the whole thing –"

There was something terribly earnest and manful in Eddie now; this was not insolence but despair. With a stab of hope the priest noticed for the first time a quiver on the twisted lips.

"Father Flanagan, you're a phony!"

"You better prove that, Eddie – or shut up!"

"Okay! I just kicked a sister in the shins. Now what do you say?"

"I still say you are a good boy."

"What did I tell you? You keep on saying that lie and you know it's a lie. It can't be true. Don't that prove you're a phony?"

Dear Heavenly Father, this is his honest logic! How can I answer it? How defend my faith in him – and in You? Because it's now or never with Eddie – God give me the grace to say the right thing.

Father Flanagan cleared his throat.

"Eddie, you're smart enough to know when a thing is really proved. What is a good boy? A good boy is an obedient boy. Right?"

"Yeah!"

"Always does what teachers tell him to do?"

"Yeah!"

"Well, that's all you've ever done, Eddie. The only trouble is that you had the wrong teachers – wharf toughs and corner bums. But you certainly obeyed them. You've done every wrong and rotten thing they taught you to do. If you would only obey the good teachers here in the same way, you'd be just fine!"

Those simple words of unarguable truth were like an exorcism, driving out devils from the room and cleansing the air. At first the tiny human enigma looked dumfounded. Then came a glisten of sheer, downright relief in the brown eyes, and he edged around the side of the sunlit desk. And with the very same relief Father Flanagan's soul was crying; he held out his arms and the child climbed into them and laid a tearful face against his heart.

That was a long time ago. For ten years Eddie remained in Boys Town. Then, well near the top of his class, he left to join the United States Marines. On blood-smeared beaches he won three promotions.

"His chest," boasts Father Flanagan, "is covered with decorations. Nothing strange about that, for he has plenty of courage. But God be praised for something else: he had the love of the men in his outfit – brother to the whole bunch. He is an upstanding Christian character. And still the toughest kid I ever knew!"

The Gift of Understanding

The confidence of childhood is a fragile thing. It can be preserved or destroyed in an instant...

I must have been about four years old when I first entered Mr. Wigden's sweet shop, but the smell of that wonderful world of penny treasures still comes back to me clearly more than half a century later. Whenever he heard the tiny tinkle of the bell attached to the front door, Mr. Wigden quietly appeared to take his stand behind the counter. he was very old, and his head was topped with a cloud of fine, snow-white hair.

Never was such an array of delicious temptations spread before a child. It was almost painful to make a choice. Each kind had first to be savoured in the imagination before passing on to the next. There was always a short pang of regret as the selection was dropped into a little white paper bag. Perhaps another kind would taste better? Or last longer? Mr. Wigden had a trick of scooping your selection into the bag, then pausing. Not a word was spoken, but every child understood that Mr. Wigden's raised eyebrows constituted a last-minute opportunity to make an exchange. Only after payment was laid upon the counter was the bag irrevocably twisted shut and the moment of indecision ended.

Our house was two streets away from the tram-line, and you had to pass the shop going to and from the trams. Mother had taken me into town on some forgotten errand,

and as we walked home from the tram she turned into Mr. Wigden's.

"Let's see if we can find something good," she said, leading me up to the long glass case as the old man approached from behind a curtained aperture. My mother stood talking to him for a few minutes as I gazed rapturously at the display before my eyes. Then Mother chose something for me and paid Mr. Wigden.

Mother went into town once or twice a week, and, since in those days baby-sitters were almost unheard-of, I usually accompanied her. It became a regular routine for her to take me into the sweet shop for some special treat, and after that first visit I was always allowed to make my own choice.

I knew nothing of money at that time. I would watch my mother hand something to people, who would then hand her a package or a bag, and slowly the idea of exchange percolated into my mind. Some time about then I reached a decision. I would travel the interminable two streets to Mr. Wigden's all alone. I remember the tinkle of the bell as I managed, after some considerable effort, to push open the big door. Enthralled, I worked my way slowly down the display counter.

Here were spearmint leaves with a fresh minty fragrance. There, gumdrops – the great big ones, so tender to bite into, all crusty with crystals of sugar. I couldn't pass by the satin cushions, little hard squares filled with sherbet. In

"Reprinted with permission from September 1965 Reader's Digest
© 1965 The Reader's Digest"

the next tray were coloured jelly-babies. The box behind them held gobstoppers which were enormous, made a most satisfying bulge in your cheek, and lasted at least an hour if you didn't roll them round in your mouth too much, or take them out too often to see what colour layer was exposed at the moment.

The hard, shiny, dark-brown-covered nuts Mr. Wigden dished out with a little wooden scoop – two scoops for a penny. And, of course, there were liquorice all sorts. These lasted a longtime, too, if you nibbled them slowly, and let the bites dissolve instead of chewing them up.

When I had picked out a promising assortment and several little white paper bags were standing on top of the counter, Mr. Wigden leaned over and asked, "You have the money to pay for all these?"

"Oh, yes," I replied, "I have lots of money." I reached out my fist, and into Mr. Widgen's open hand I dumped half a dozen cherry-stones carefully wrapped in silver-paper.

Mr. Widgen stood gazing at the palm of his hand; then he looked searchingly at me for a long moment.

"Isn't it enough?" I asked him anxiously.

He sighed gently. "I think it is a bit too much," he answered.

"You've got some change to come." He walked over to his old-fashioned cash register and cranked open the drawer. Returning to the counter, he leaned over and dropped two pennies into my outstretched hand.

My mother scolded me about going all that way alone when she found me out. I don't think it ever occurred to her to ask about the financial arrangement. I was simply cautioned not to go again unless I asked first. I must have obeyed, and evidently, when permission was granted for

me to go again, a penny or two was given to me for my purchases, since I don't remember using cherry-stones a second time. In fact, the affair, insignificant to me then, was soon forgotten in the busy occupation of growing up.

When I was six or seven years old my family moved to another town, where I grew up, eventually married and established my own family. My wife and I opened a shop where we bred and sold tropical fish. The acquarium trade was then still in its infancy, and most of the fish were imported from Africa and South America. Few species sold for less then five dollars a pair.

One sunny afternoon a little girl came in accompanied by her brother. They were perhaps five and six years old. I was busy cleaning the tanks. The two children stood with wide, round eyes, staring at the jewelled beauties swimming in the crystal-clear water. "Gosh," exclaimed the boy, "can we buy some?"

"Yes," I replied. "If you can pay for them."

"Oh, we have lots of money," the little girl said confidently.

Something in the way she spoke gave me an odd feeling of familiarity. After watching the fish for some time they asked me for pairs of several different kinds, pointing them out as they walked down the row of tanks. I netted their choices into a travelling container and slipped it into an insulated bag for transport, handing it to the boy. "Carry it carefully," I cautioned.

He nodded and turned to his sister. "You pay him," he said. I held out my hand, and as her clenched fist approached me I suddenly knew exactly what was going to happen, even what the little girl was going to say. Her fist opened, and into my outstretched palm she dumped three small coins.

In that instant I sensed the full impact of the legacy Mr. Wigden had given me so many years before. Only now did I recognize the challenge I had presented to the old man, and realize how wonderfully he had met it.

I seemed to be standing again in the little sweet shop as I looked at the coins in my own hand. I understood the innocence of the two children and the power to preserve or destroy that innocence, as Mr. Wigden had understood those long years ago. I was so filled up with the remembering that my throat ached. The little girl was standing expectantly before me. "Isn't it enough?" she asked in a small voice.

"It's a little too much," I managed to say over the lump in my throat. "You've got some change to come." I rummaged round in the cash drawer, dropped two cents into her open hand, then stood in the doorway watching the children walk away, carefully carrying their treasure.

When I went back into the shop, my wife was standing on a stool with her arms submerged to the elbows in a tank where she was rearranging the plants. "What was that all about?" she asked. "Do you know how many fish you gave them?"

"About 30 dollars' worth," I answered, the lump still in my throat. "But I couldn't have done anything else."

When I had finished telling her about old Mr. Wigden, her eyes were wet, and she stepped off the stool and gave me a gentle kiss on the cheek.

"I still smell the gumdrops," I sighed, and I'm certain I heard old Mr. Wigden chuckle over my shoulder as I wiped down the last tank.

ACKNOWLEDGMENTS :

Our grateful thanks to the following :

1) *Sri Aurobindo Ashram Trust for*
   a) *The writings and photographs of Sri Aurobindo and the Mother*
   b) *Photographs and paintings of the Ashram artistes*
2) *The Reader's Digest for the two articles*
   a) *Father Flanagan's Toughest Customer*
   b) *A Gift of Understanding*
3) *The Vedanta Society of Southern California for their translation of the Chandogya Upanishad by Swami Prabhavananda and Frederick Manchester*
4) *Pondicherry International Salon of Photography, Sri Aurobindo Ashram, Pondicherry, for the following photographs*
   a) *Cover _ Karp Grigoryevich (USSR)*
   b) *Page 27 _ Dobelis Edmunds (USSR)*
   c) *Page 35 _ Yu-Chiu Cheung (Hong Kong)*
   d) *Page 37 _ Koulatsoglou Constantin (Greece)*
   e) *Page 47 _ Alois H. Bernkopf (Austria)*
   f) *Page 57 _ Karl Vock Junior (Austria)*
   g) *Page 58 _ Dr. Weissenbock (Coa Wienn)*

REFERENCES

Page	Source
7	*Sri Aurobindo Birth Centenary Library* (Vol. 15), p. 605
8	*Collected Works of the Mother* (Vol. 2), pp. 153-54
10	*Ibid.* (Vol. 12), p. 9
11	*Ibid.* (Vol. 12), pp. 9-11
12	*Ibid.* (Vol. 5), pp. 413-14
13	*Ibid.* (Vol. 12), pp. 16-17
14	*Ibid.* (Vol. 12), pp. 12-13; pp. 13-14
15	*Ibid.* (Vol. 12), pp. 15-16
16	*Ibid.* (Vol. 5), p. 296
17	*Ibid.* (Vol. 12), pp. 14-15
18	*Ibid.* (Vol. 12), p. 15; (Vol. 9), p. 80
20	*Ibid.* (Vol. 12), p. 168; p. 389; p. 360; pp. 194-95
21	*Sri Aurobindo Birth Centenary Library* (Vol. 17), p. 215
21	*Collected Works of the Mother* (Vol. 12), p. 171
22	*Ibid.* (Vol. 12), p. 170; p. 171; pp. 406-07
23	*Ibid.* (Vol. 12), p. 407
24	*Ibid.* (Vol. 8), p. 182; (Vol. 12), p. 167; p. 167
25	*Ibid.* (Vol. 12), pp. 155-56; p. 152; pp. 404-05
26	*Ibid.* (Vol. 7), pp. 286-87; (Vol. 8), pp. 180-81
27	*Ibid.* (Vol. 8), pp. 182-84
30	*Ibid.* (Vol. 12), p. 196; p. 184; p. 191; (Vol. 8), pp. 180-81; (Vol. 12), p. 153
32	*Ibid.* (Vol. 12), p. 135; p. 134; p. 136; p. 369
33	*Ibid.* (Vol. 12), p. 368; pp. 25-26
34	*Ibid.* (Vol. 6), pp. 151-52
36	*Ibid.* (Vol. 12), p. 169; p. 370; pp. 154-55; p. 144; p. 147
37	*Ibid.* (Vol. 4), p. 28; (Vol. 12), p. 11
38	*Ibid.* (Vol. 12), p. 364; p. 197; p. 196; pp. 379-80
39	*Ibid.* (Vol. 4), pp. 24-25
40	*Ibid.* (Vol. 4), pp. 26-27
42	*Ibid.* (Vol. 4), pp. 23-24
43	*Ibid.* (Vol. 6), pp. 411-15
46	*Ibid.* (Vol. 12), pp. 436-39